Thomas Cook

Cook's Cruise to the Mediterranean, the Orient and Bible Lands

weitsuechtig

Thomas Cook

Cook's Cruise to the Mediterranean, the Orient and Bible Lands

ISBN/EAN: 9783943850260

Auflage: 1

Erscheinungsjahr: 2012

Erscheinungsort: Bremen, Deutschland

@ weitsuechtig in Access Verlag GmbH, Fahrenheitstr. 1, 28359 Bremen. Alle Rechte beim Verlag und bei den jeweiligen Lizenzgebern.

weitsuechtig

SECOND EDITION

COOK'S CRUISE

TO THE

MEDITERRANEAN, THE ❧ ❧

ORIENT AND BIBLE LANDS

by the magnificent new Hamburg-American Line Twin-Screw Steamship "MOLTKE" (12,000 tons), specially chartered for this Cruise by THOS. COOK & SON,

—— VISITING ——

Madeira, Gibraltar, Algiers, Malta, Athens, Constantinople, Smyrna (for Ephesus), Beyrout (for Damascus), Haifa (for Galilee), Jaffa (for Jerusalem, Bethlehem, etc.), Alexandria, Cairo, the Nile (optional), Naples (Pompeii, Vesuvius, Rome, etc.), Nice, Monte Carlo, etc.

With several attractive Optional Return Routes across Europe.

A GRAND 70-DAY CRUISE,

Leaving New York on Wednesday, February 4, 1903,

AT THE LOWEST FARES EVER
OFFERED FOR HIGH-CLASS TRAVEL,

Including Shore Excursions, Hotels, Carriage Drives, Guides, Fees, etc.

ARRANGED AND MANAGED THROUGHOUT BY

THOS. COOK & SON,

Managers of Tours and Excursions, and Universal Steamship and Railroad Ticket Agents.

By Royal Appointment Passenger Agents for the Royal British Commission, Vienna, 1873; Philadelphia, 1876; Paris, 1878; Colonial and Indian, 1886; Chicago, 1893, and Paris, 1900, etc. Sole owners of the new first-class Tourist and Express Steamers, specially built for the Nile. International Passenger Agents, under special appointment, to the Italian, Indian and Australasian Railways. General Passenger Agents for the Midland Railway of England, and Official Ticket Agents for the Trunk Lines and Principal Railroads of America, etc., etc.

NEW YORK, 261 and 1185 Broadway.   BOSTON, 332 Washington St.
PHILADELPHIA, 828 Chestnut St.   CHICAGO, 234 South Clark St.
SAN FRANCISCO, 621 Market Street.

London, Paris, Rome, Cairo, Jerusalem, Bombay, Melbourne, etc.

ESTABLISHED 1841.

TC & S—No. 21—M, 1902.

THE NEW HAMBURG-AMERICAN LINE TWIN-SCREW STEAMSHIP "MOLTKE" (12,000 TONS).
The most luxurious ocean steamship afloat.

CONTENTS.

	Page.
Map of the Cruise	4
Epitome of the Itinerary, Mileage, etc.	5
Introductory	7
Description of Cruise, Steamer and Arrangements	9-19
Fare and Conditions	19
Notes for Members	21-25
Daily Itinerary of Main Tour	27-45
Optional Extension Tours on the Nile	47-57
Optional Side Trips in the Holy Land	59-65
Optional Tours Across Europe	67-79

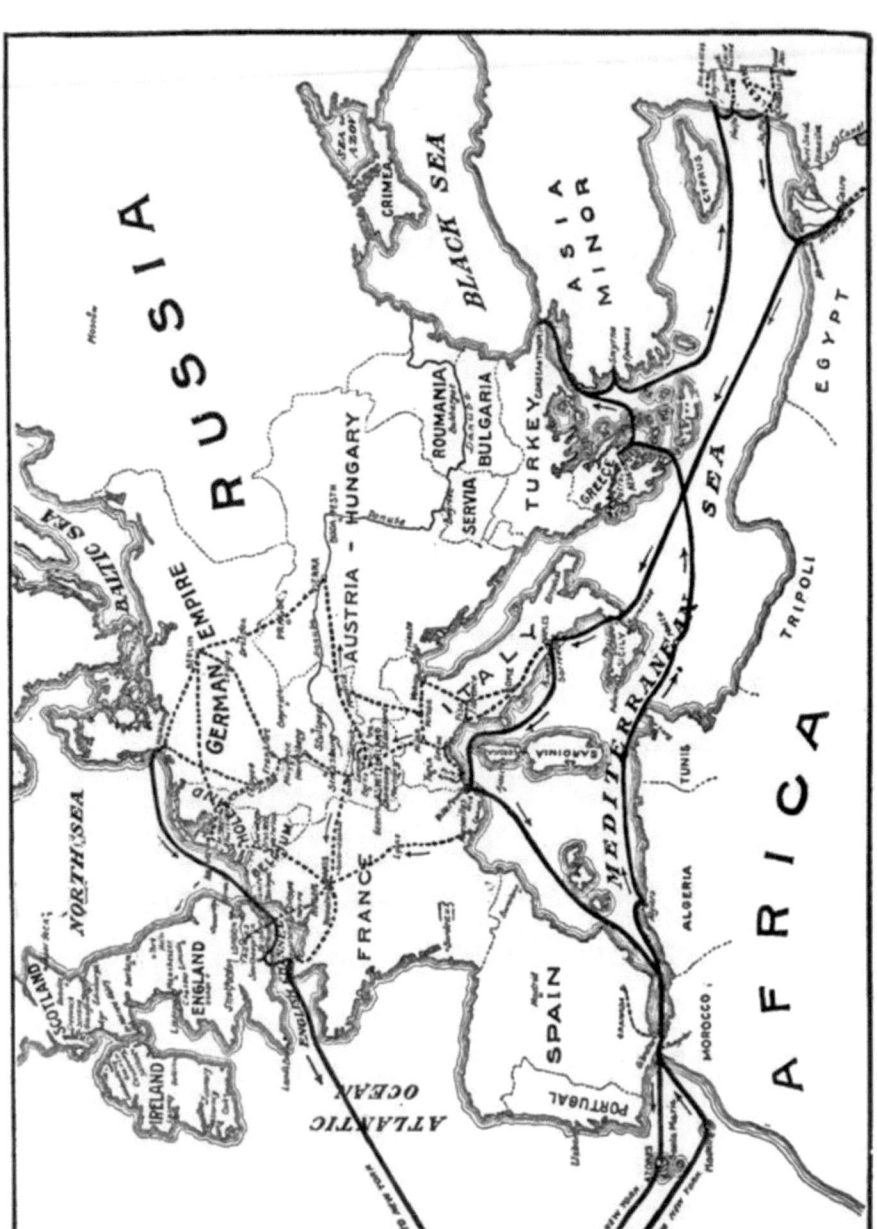

MAP OF COOK'S "MOLTKE" CRUISE, 1903.

ITINERARY OF THE CRUISE.

LEAVE NEW YORK, WED. FEB. 4, 1903	MILES	ARRIVAL ABOUT	DEPARTURE ABOUT	STAY days	STAY hours
New York....	....	....	Wed. Feb. 4, 11 a.m		
Funchal, Madeira....	2760	Thurs. Feb. 12, 12 noon..	Fri. Feb. 13, 2 p.m.....	1	2
Gibraltar....	618	Sun. Feb. 15, 8 a.m......	Mon. Feb. 16, 12 m'dn't.	1	16
Excursion by special train to Granada (the Alhambra) and return.					
Algiers....	382				
Valetta, Malta....	410	Wed. Feb. 18, 7 a.m.....	Thurs. Feb. 19, 5 p.m.....	1	10
to Citta Vecchia and return....	573	Sat. Feb. 21, 9 a.m.....	Sat. Feb. 21, 7 p.m.....		10
Piraeus, for Athens....	20	During stay at Malta.			
to Athens and return, two excursions by rail....	470	Mon. Feb. 23, 7 a.m.....	Tues. Feb. 24, 5 p.m....	1	10
Constantinople....	29	During stay at Piraeus.			
excursion up the Bosphorus to the Black Sea and return, continuing to....	356	Wed. Feb. 25, 5 p.m.....	Sat. Feb. 28, 10 a.m.....	2	17
Smyrna, for Ephesus....	24	Sun. Mar. 1, 7 a.m	Sun. Mar. 1, 5 p.m.....		
Beyrout, for Damascus excursion....	295	Tues. Mar. 3, 1 p.m.....	Tues. Mar. 3, 12 m'dn't..		
Haifa, for Galilee and Samaria tour....	640	Wed. Mar. 4, 6 a.m.....	Wed. Mar. 4, 8 a.m.....		
Jaffa....	72	Wed. Mar. 4, 12 noon....	Wed. Mar. 4, 5 p.m.....		10
excursion to Jerusalem, Bethlehem, etc....	54	Option of 5 or 12 days in the Holy Land.			
Beyrout, Damascus section embarks....	120	Thurs. Mar. 5, 7 a.m....	Sun. Mar. 8, 9 a m		
Haifa, Galilee section embarks....	124				
Jaffa, land Damascus and Galilee sections and embark section for 12 days Egyptian tour....	72	Sun. Mar. 8, 2 p.m......	Mon. Mar. 9, 2 a m		
Alexandria, land section for 12 days Egyptian tour,....	54	Mon. Mar. 9, 7 a.m......	Mon. Mar. 9, 1 p.m.....	19	2
excursion by rail to Cairo, Pyramids, etc....	267	Tues. Mar. 10, 7 a.m.....	Sat. Mar. 14, 10 a.m....		
Jaffa....	240	Option of 5 or 12 days in Egypt.			
Alexandria, land section for 5 days Egyptian tour....	267	Sun. Mar. 15, 7 a.m.....	Mon. Mar. 16, 1 p.m.....		
Naples....	267	Tues. Mar. 17, 8 a.m....	Sun. Mar. 22, 8 p.m.....	5	10
excursion to Pompeii, Rome, etc., by rail	1040	Wed. Mar. 25, 12 noon...	Mon. Mar. 30, 10 p.m....		
Villefranche (Nice), excursion to Nice and Monte Carlo....	380	Passengers have 2 days in Naples, 3 days in Rome.			
	360	{Wed. Apl. 1, or Thurs. Apl. 2, 7 a.m.... or	Thurs. Apl. 2, or Fri. Apl. 3, 12 m'dn't....}	1	17
New York....	3800	{Tues. Apl. 14, or Wed. Apl. 15, 6 a.m......			
Total	13665				

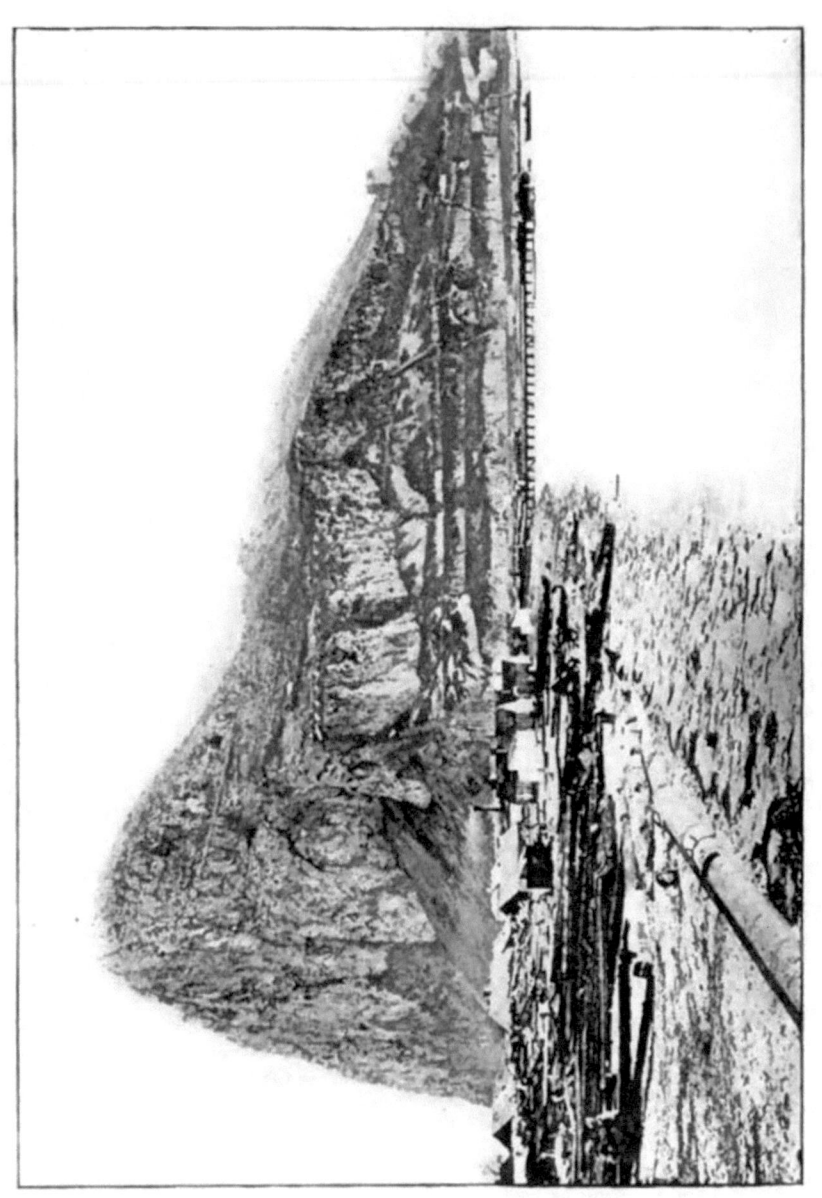

GIBRALTAR.

INTRODUCTORY.

THE MOST approved form of high-class pleasure travel to-day is undoubtedly the Yachting Cruise. Properly managed, it represents the latest development of modern luxury and convenience, and the fullest application of organization and co-operation in travel. It is typical "Twentieth Century" travel, in that it renders accessible to the many what was for years the exclusive privilege of the wealthy few. It possesses, among many obvious advantages, the important one of permitting the voyager to assume at pleasure, or as the occasion may demand, the *role* of one of a numerous company of fellow-travelers, or of a member of a smaller and private section of the same, or to be simply an individual passenger on a well-filled Ocean steamship.

The Oriental Cruise described in the following pages embodies all the best features and most recent advances in this delightful mode of travel. The region to be visited—the Mediterranean and adjacent European and Oriental countries—is pre-eminently adapted to the conditions of such a tour, full of strong contrasts and varied attractions. We have specially chartered for the Cruise a steamship peculiarly suited to the purpose, and bring to the preparation and management of the undertaking an experience of SIXTY-ONE YEARS in this business, and a world-wide organization and equipment. We call attention to this here, because it is only our superior and exclusive facilities which have enabled us to offer the very complete Cruise itself for so small a price, and to make the extraordinarily moderate charges for the Optional Extensions and Side Trips.

Thos. Cook & Son.

S. S. "MOLTKE."—PROMENADE DECK.

THE CRUISE.

The regions to be visited in the course of this Cruise are among the most beautiful, varied and interesting in the world. Along the shores of the sunny Mediterranean, where the Phœnician galleys crept from point to point in man's earliest efforts at navigation, our voyagers will sail in one of the finest examples of modern maritime construction yet produced, to visit lands famous in history and mythology, celebrated for their scenic beauty, the momentous events that have transpired within their borders, the wonderful relics of past ages they contain, and the treasures of ancient and modern art stored in their great cities. The tourists will see the great modern fortresses of Gibraltar and Malta; at Algiers, Constantinople and Cairo mingle with the picturesque life of the strange Mohammedan world in those mysterious Oriental countries that seem to have remained unchanged since the days of Saladin and Haroun Al Raschid; in the Holy Land tread the self-same paths and view the same hills and valleys and cities as the Patriarchs and Apostles, and dwell for a time among the actual scenes of the Sacred Story. In Rome and Athens they will visit the beautiful and astonishing remains of the classical world; in Egypt and on the Nile the stupendous Pyramids and marvellous pictured Temples. Tombs and ruined cities many thousands of years old, while at Nice and Monte Carlo—the gems of the beautiful

AN ORIENTAL TYPE.

S. S. "MOLTKE."—ONE OF THE DINING ROOMS.

Riviera, and the Winter playground of the *elite* of European Society —the luxury, gaiety and brilliance of the modern world are seen at their height.

The whole time will be spent in the perfect Winter climate of the Mediterranean, a season when most of the region is bright with flowers and luxuriant foliage; when skies are always blue, the air balmy and health-giving; the weather, in fact, enjoyed here in early summer. The members will thus escape the worst of our Northern Winter, with its ice and snow and bitter winds, and generally uncomfortable accompaniments.

THE S. S. "MOLTKE,"

which we have specially chartered from the Hamburg American Line, is a new and magnificent example of the modern palatial Ocean liner, and fully maintains the high standard of construction and equipment which has always distinguished the Hamburg American Line, and enabled that famous organization to attain its present position as the largest Steamship Company of the world. The dimensions of the "Moltke" are: Length, 525 feet; width, 62 feet; depth, 45 feet. The hull is divided into numerous water-tight compartments, and provided with a double bottom, features that add greatly to the security of the vessel, while her large bilge keels give unusual steadiness at sea, and almost entirely obviate "rolling" and the accompanying seasickness. The twin screws are driven by two sets of quadruple expansion engines of great power.

The passenger accommodation is not only decorated and furnished in a most elaborate and artistic manner, but possesses several novel features of great value. One of these is the fine

GYMNASIUM,

fully equipped with modern apparatus of every kind, including mechanical massage apparatus. On an extended voyage this opportunity of obtaining suitable exercise will be much appreciated, and will materially assist in making the time pass pleasantly.

SPORTS.

In addition to the attractions of the Gymnasium, which will be always at the disposal of the passengers, a number of athletic events and contests for the passengers will take place, numerous *gymkhana* being arranged. These will be managed and controlled by a committee of the passengers.

S. S. "MOLTKE."—THE GRILL ROOM.

THE GRILL ROOM

will be a great attraction to those who may wish to dine when they please, or who may not feel well enough on stormy days to go to the dining saloon. At the head of the main companionway there is a large

HOTEL OFFICE AND POST OFFICE,

or steward's office, which must prove a great convenience to passengers during the Cruise.

SHELTERED CORNERS

are provided on the Promenade and Boat Decks, so that in the unlikely event of rough weather being encountered, the passengers may take the fresh air in comfort, and these corners have been beautifully furnished with palms and other fresh foliage plants. The

SALOONS AND SMOKING ROOMS,

and all the other spacious apartments are most luxuriously furnished, and were designed to afford ample accommodation for a much larger number of passengers than will accompany this Cruise.

THE STATEROOMS

are all unusually large, and the most thoughtful consideration has been displayed to make them thoroughly comfortable and homelike. Their equipment is complete, down to such details as electric curling-irons for ladies, and electric food-warmers for invalids and children. A large number of the rooms have lower berths only, many of them may be arranged *en suite* for the use of families or friends, and there are a number of Chambres de Luxe, with private bath and toilet. Many of the staterooms have been fitted for the sole use of one person only. There are no less than

THIRTY BATH ROOMS

on the "Moltke" provided with all the latest improvements, such as hot and cold showers.

S. S. "MOLTKE."—THE GYMNASIUM.

CUISINE, ETC.

The Hamburg American Line is celebrated for the superior excellence of its Cuisine, and for this Cruise a most elaborate and bountiful table will be provided, amply supplied with all the delicacies of the season. Cigars, wines, beers and mineral waters may be had on board, of the first quality, at moderate prices.

It would be possible, did space permit, to mention many more attractions and advantages to be found on board the "Moltke," but enough has been said to justify our statement that for this Cruise we have chartered one of

THE MOST LUXURIOUS OCEAN STEAMSHIPS AFLOAT.

And this magnificent vessel will be absolutely at the service of the party for the entire Cruise.

To add to the comfort of the members and to avoid overcrowding, the

NUMBER OF PASSENGERS IS LIMITED

to the ordinary cabin stateroom capacity of the vessel. The "Moltke" has comfortably carried across the Atlantic on one voyage no less than 2,500 passengers, but for this Cruise only about 500 passengers will be taken, all being accommodated in the permanent cabin staterooms. All the spacious saloon and deck accommodations, designed for a large number of passengers, will be entirely at the service of the comparatively small number of passengers carried on this Cruise. Experienced travelers will appreciate the additional comfort conferred by this exceptional arrangement. The passengers for this Cruise are not to be regarded as one large party, but to promote to the utmost their comfort and convenience, will be arranged in many small parties or sections, which may be made up according to the wishes of the members. In many parts of the country, special sections are being locally organized —congenial acquaintances and neighbors are planning to travel in company. The ladies and gentlemen composing these sections will be assigned, as far as possible, to adjacent staterooms and seats at table, also accommodated at the same hotels.

S. S. "MOLTKE."—ONE OF THE SMOKING ROOMS.

PERSONAL MANAGEMENT.

The "Moltke" is specially chartered by THOS. COOK & SON, and the Cruise will be managed throughout by them. The whole of the arrangements are being managed and supervised throughout by the American Manager, assisted by a competent staff of Conductors and Interpreters. In Egypt and Palestine all the plans will be carried out by the Resident Managers, men who have lived continuously on the spot for many years, and fully understand the languages and characteristics of the peoples. The whole of the immense equipment owned by THOS. COOK & SON will be at the disposal of members of the Cruise, both in Egypt and Palestine, thus insuring suitable accommodations, that cannot otherwise be obtained. Some idea of our facilities in Palestine may be obtained from the several illustrations in this pamphlet, from photographs taken in that country. THOS. COOK & SON maintain their own offices everywhere throughout the Mediterranean, the East and Europe, in which respect they stand alone. In Egypt they own and operate a large fleet of large and elegantly equipped steamers, specially built for the Nile service. In Palestine they maintain a large permanent staff and immense equipment for managing travel by either camp, carriages, or rail where available.

TO SECURE MEMBERSHIP.

Already a very large number of berths have been applied for, and in order to secure passage, immediate application should be made, with full name and address, and a deposit of $10 per passenger. On receipt thereof a Deposit Receipt will be sent, with plan of the steamer, showing berth allotted. On November 1 a further payment of $40 per passenger must be made, and the balance of the passage money must be paid by January 5, 1903. The staterooms are graded according to desirability of location, size, and number of passengers to occupy them, as on all Ocean steamers. The higher priced rooms are better located and more commodious, and are more elegantly equipped, but all the passengers have the same deck and saloon privileges. As the staterooms of each category are allotted strictly according to priority of application, an

IMMEDIATE SELECTION

is very advantageous. The small deposit required to secure a berth makes this an easy matter.

S. S. "MOLTKE."—THE SOCIAL HALL.

STATEROOMS AND SEATS AT TABLE

will be assigned for the entire Cruise.

OPTIONAL SIDE TRIPS.

In addition to the very complete Itinerary of the Cruise, we have planned a number of attractive side trips in the HOLY LAND, on THE NILE and in EUROPE. These are offered at unprecedentedly low fares, such as have never before been available in these countries, and ample time is allowed for these extra Tours being carried out in a most comfortable and satisfactory manner. As already stated, the unique facilities possessed by THOS. COOK & SON throughout the East and Europe make it possible to offer our patrons superior and exclusive advantages, both as regards fares and character of accommodation provided.

The steamer makes two trips between Jaffa and Alexandria (see Itinerary on page 37), so that passengers have the choice of spending five days in Palestine and twelve in Egypt, or *vice versa*.

TO RETURN ACROSS EUROPE.

For members wishing to combine a short Continental Tour of Europe with this Oriental Cruise, a special series of short tours has been arranged, full particulars of which will be found in this pamphlet.

VALIDITY OF TICKETS.

Passengers have the option of returning by any steamship of the Hamburg-American Line, including the famous "Deutschland," one of the fastest ocean steamships in the world; the "Fürst Bismarck," "Auguste Victoria," "Columbia," etc., at any time previous to August 1, 1903, the accommodation furnished being of the same character as that occupied on the "Moltke." Any passengers desiring to remain over later than August 1 can do so at their leisure, subject to the payment of a slight additional charge in the event of their returning during the height of the season. This to be arranged in Europe.

RATE OF FARE FOR 70-DAY CRUISE, $300 and Upwards.

Since the first announcement was made, there has been such an instantaneous and widespread demand for accommodation, that all the berths at $300, $350 and $375 have

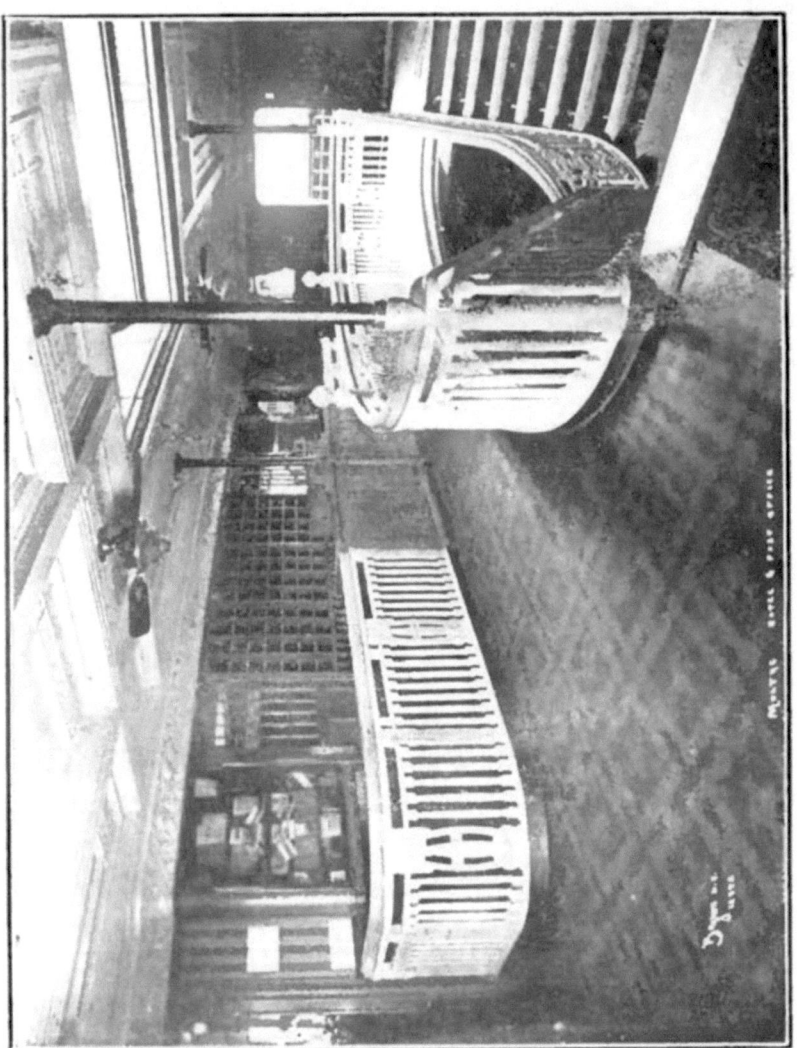

S. S. "MOLTKE."—HOTEL OFFICE AND POST OFFICE.

been reserved, and deposits accepted. Should any of these passengers withdraw, the berths will be again placed on sale. In the meantime, there is ample accommodation at $400 and upwards. On application a plan will be sent, showing location and price of every stateroom on the ship.

THE FARE INCLUDES

1. Steamship and railway tickets for the entire route.
2. Full accommodation on board the "Moltke" in accordance with the well-known and luxurious service of the Hamburg American Line. Hotel accommodation on shore, where indicated in the Itinerary, consisting of three meals per day.
3. Transfers to and from stations, piers, hotels, etc., where necessary.
4. Fees for sightseeing mentioned in Itinerary, porterage, and all traveling expenses, except the steward's fee on the steamer, which is an entirely personal matter, and cannot be included.
5. Services of local guides, interpreters, dragomans, etc., where necessary, and the services of COOK'S representatives and Conductors throughout the Cruise.
6. Landing and embarkation at ports of Madeira, Gibraltar, Algiers, Malta, Piræus, Constantinople, Smyrna, Beyrout, Jaffa, Haifa, Alexandria, Naples and Villefranche.
7. Carriage drives at Alexandria, Cairo, the Pyramids, Jerusalem to Bethlehem, the Pools of Solomon, Mount of Olives, Gethsemane and Bethany, Naples, and one entire day in Rome.
8. Shore Excursions, as per Itinerary, from Gibraltar to Granada, the Alhambra and return; Valetta, Malta, to Citta Vecchia and return; Alexandria to Cairo and return; Jaffa to Jerusalem, Bethlehem and return; Piræus to Athens (two days), Naples, Pompeii and Rome; Villefranche to Nice and Monte Carlo and return.

NOTES FOR MEMBERS.

BAGGAGE.—Our Conductors and representatives look after all baggage, except hand-baggage. Each passenger is allowed twenty cubic feet (about 300 lbs.) of personal baggage on the steamer, and the free conveyance of 56 lbs. in Europe. For the Jerusalem, Cairo and Rome excursions, each passenger is allowed two valises and a dress-suit case.

S. S. "MOLTKE."—ONE OF THE STATEROOMS.

Ladies spending twelve days in Palestine or Egypt will be allowed one trunk or two valises. No trunks will be taken up the Nile.

On board the steamer a baggage room will be provided for large trunks, to which daily access will be allowed. All articles required during the voyage should be carried in a steamer trunk, which must not exceed fourteen inches in height, so that it may go under the berth.

All trunks and hand baggage must have tags attached, showing name of passenger, and number of stateroom; proper tags will be furnished by us for this purpose. Baggage may be sent to the Hamburg Piers, foot of First Street, Hoboken, two days before sailing, where it will be placed in the baggage room, *and not sent on board until claimed by the passenger before embarking.* Out-of-town passengers arriving in New York can have their baggage checked to the pier by the express baggage agent on the train, but ample time must be allowed.

While anxious to render all possible assistance to travelers in the transport, care and checking of baggage, THOS. COOK & SON are not responsible in cases of detention, damage to or loss of baggage. In all cases of transference, each article of baggage must be identified by its owner, especially on entering and leaving hotels and railway stations, and whenever baggage is subject to Customs examination its owner must be present. Small packages, such as handbags, umbrellas, traveling rugs, etc., must remain entirely under the control of the owner.

EXTRA FUNDS.—The safest and most convenient manner in which to carry funds for any intended purchases, is by means of CIRCULAR NOTES, issued at any of the offices of THOS. COOK & SON in America. The cost is but 50 cents per $100; they are cashed at upwards of one thousand places by banks, hotels, etc., and in case of loss, payment may be stopped and the money recovered. THOS. COOK & SON also issue LETTERS OF CREDIT and make cable transfers, and have on hand foreign money of the various countries of Europe for sale at current rates.

PASSPORTS.—Passports with *vise* of the Turkish Consul are necessary, and can be obtained through us at a cost of $3.00, including *vise*. In making application state whether you are a native-born or naturalized citizen. One passport is sufficient for a man and wife and minor

PALESTINE.—INTERIOR OF ONE OF COOK'S PAVILIONS, AS PROVIDED FOR H. I. M. THE EMPEROR OF GERMANY.

children. Passengers taking the Galilee or Samaria trip also require a Turkish *tazkarah*, or local passport, which will cost $1.60, a form for which will be sent.

CLOTHING.—The tourist should be governed by his ordinary custom in this matter. Many ladies and gentlemen dress for dinner on board ship, also at hotels at Cairo and elsewhere, but this is not obligatory. For the Atlantic voyage warm clothing is necessary, also steamer rug for the deck. For use on shore, ordinary Spring or Fall clothing, with both light and heavy underclothes; one or two good pairs of shoes.

STEAMER CHAIRS.—Steamer chairs may be hired from Thos. Cook & Son for the Cruise at a cost of $2.00. This must be arranged when booking.

INSTRUCTIONS FOR FORWARDING MAIL will be sent to passengers before sailing, printed for the use of friends at home, who will also be advised by postal card of the safe arrival of the steamer at the principal ports, if a proper address is registered before sailing.

SPECIAL NOTICE.

In the event of the Managers (Thos. Cook & Son) or the Owners (The Hamburg-American Line) considering it advisable in their discretion to withdraw the steamer on account of the imposition of quarantine or any other cause, the full amounts paid shall be returned, and upon the tendering of the same the firm and ship shall be free from all liability.

Neither the Managers nor the Owners are responsible for loss of time or money consequent on the irregularity of steamboat or railway service, quarantine, sickness, or any calamity or hindrance (Acts of God) caused by circumstances over which they have no control; and should delays or alterations occur through these, the passengers will have to pay any additional necessary expenses for living and accommodation in hotels or on steamers which may be incurred beyond the specified period.

Should these or any other circumstances make it necessary to omit one or more of the ports of call mentioned in the Itinerary, the Managers and Owners shall be free from all liability in respect of such omissions. These, however, are very remote contingencies, but should they occur the judgment of the Captain of the ship must be accepted as final.

MOSLEMS AT PRAYER.

DAILY ITINERARY

OF THE

MAIN TOUR.

Wednesday, February 4, 1903.—Leave **New York** at 11 A. M. by the Hamburg-American Line new twin-screw steamship "Moltke," the most luxuriously appointed 12,000-ton steamship afloat. *(Steamer sails from Hamburg Piers, foot of First Street, Hoboken. Passengers should take the Barclay Street or Christopher Street Ferry from New York.)*

The steamer follows a southerly course, through the warm and pleasant expanse of the South Atlantic Ocean, the bitter winter weather of New York being soon exchanged for a mild and exhilarating temperature and brilliant skies. The superb service and many attractions on board the "Moltke" make the eight-day voyage to Madeira, the first port touched at, a delightful and beneficial experience, and relieve the daily life of any semblance of monotony.

FUNCHAL, MADEIRA.

MADEIRA.

Thursday, February 12, and Friday, February 13.—At **Madeira**, where the steamer remains about 26 hours. Funchal, the port of call, is the capital of these fertile and beautiful islands, which belong to the Kingdom of Portugal. The scenery is magnificent and varied, though chiefly mountainous in character. Owing to the steepness of the roads, sledges, drawn by bullocks, take the place of wheeled vehicles, of which there are none on the islands. Other modes of locomotion are hammocks and basket sledges, the latter being used for descending the mountains, skilfully guided by a runner behind. Madeira is noted for its flowers and fruit, and also for basket-work, embroidery, lace shawls, gold and silver inlaid work, etc.

Leaving Funchal at 2 P. M. on Friday, the steamer proceeds to Gibraltar.

SPAIN.

Sunday, February 15, and Monday, February 16.—At **Gibraltar.** *(Cook's Office, Waterport Street.)* Gibraltar is the most picturesque and strongest fortress in the world, one of Great Britain's strongholds in the Mediterranean, the western entrance to which it guards. The highest point of the great Rock is

TRAVEL IN MADEIRA.

1,430 feet, whence a magnificent view is obtained. Two or three miles of galleries have been tunnelled through the solid rock, and batteries placed at all available points. The whole rock is honeycombed with fortifications, some of the hidden batteries being known only to a select few.

From Gibraltar a most interesting side trip is made to **Granada,** for the Alhambra. Leave Gibraltar, via Algeciras and Ronda. The country through which the railroad passes is simply charming, its bold and varied scenery being rich in cork and other woods, as well as corn, fruit and olives. **Ronda,** which is passed en route, is one of the most picturesque cities in Europe, 2,500 feet above sea level. The ancient town is divided from the modern by the Tago, a huge chasm in the mountains, 200 feet wide and 250 feet deep. **Granada,** the city of running waters and fountains, is situated on one of the loveliest plains in the world. The surrounding country abounds in beautiful scenery, and the air, even in the hottest season, is delightfully tempered by the snow-capped mountains of the Sierra Nevada. The great attraction is the **Alhambra,** a wonderful Moorish palace, whose beauties have been celebrated by all travellers, especially Washington Irving. It is situated in the midst of a noble forest, surrounded by gardens, built with sumptuous taste, and is undoubtedly the grandest monument of Arabic genius in Europe. The various Halls and Courts of the palace will be visited, among others the famous Court of the Lions, the Hall of the Abencerrages and other magnificent apartments.

SPAIN.—IN THE ALHAMBRA.

Returning to Gibraltar the party embark for Algiers.

ALGIERS.

Wednesday, February 18, and Thursday, February 19.—At **Algiers,** the capital of the French colony of Algeria. *(Cook's Office, 3 Boulevard de la Republique.)* The steamer remains 34 hours. Algiers, now one of the most popular winter cities of the Mediterranean, is a picturesque and delightful combination of Oriental life and Western comforts. The town rises in terraces of dazzling whiteness from the blue water of a beautiful bay. In its narrow streets are seen a motley population of Arabs, Berbers, Turks, Moors, Bedouins, negroes, caravans from the interior, story tellers, snake charmers and all the curious features of Oriental life, while the city contains many beautiful examples of Moorish and Byzantine architecture.

CAFÉ IN ALGIERS.

MALTA.

Saturday, February 21.—Is spent at **Malta**, another of Great Britain's fortresses, and a most interesting spot, actually and historically. *(Cook's Office, 308 Strada Reale, Valetta.)* It is supposed to have been the scene of St. Paul's shipwreck, and it contains many places and objects of great interest. From Valetta, the port of call, famous for its harbor, a visit will be made to Citta Vecchia, founded B. C. 700, the ancient capital, a city of stately palaces and crumbling Old World fortifications.

GREECE.

Monday, February 23, and Tuesday, February 24.—Arriving at **Piraeus** early on Monday, the party will proceed by rail each day to **Athens,** five miles distant, the wonderful capital of ancient and modern Greece. *(Cook's Office, Place de la Constitution.)* The places of interest in and around Athens are very numerous. The wonderful monuments of antiquity naturally form the principal attraction for visitors, and are as beautiful as extensive and famous. Among the most

ATHENS.—THE PARTHENON.

important is the world-famous Acropolis, where all the most glorious monuments of the ancient city were assembled, and where their remains still stand, a wonder to all time. Two of the finest and best preserved monuments of the period immediately preceding the Christian Era are the Temples of Theseus and Jupiter Olympus. The principal places of historic interest to be visited may be briefly summarized as follows: The Acropolis, with the Parthenon, Temple of Victory and Erechtheum, the Theatre of Bacchus, Panathenaic Stadium, Temple of Archegetis, Porch of Hadrian, Temple of Theseus, Mars Hill, etc.

Wednesday, February 25.—Expect to pass through the **Dardanelles** early in the morning. On each side is an immense fort, which completely commands the strait, and near each is a handsome town—Kheled-Bahri on the European shore, and Chanak-Kalesi on the Asiatic. Above these two towns the strait expands into a sort of a bay, formed on the north by a promontory jutting out from the Asiatic shore; and upon this promontory stood old Abydos. Here Leander swam to Hero, Byron to aquatic fame, and here Xerxes laid his bridge.

CONSTANTINOPLE.—MOSQUE OF ST. SOPHIA.

TURKEY.

Wednesday, February 25, to Saturday, February 28.—At **Constantinople,** the wonderful capital of the Ottoman Empire. *(Cook's Office, 12 Rue Cabristan.)*

Constantinople proper, the Turkish Stamboul, is situated on the south side of the Golden Horn, an arm of the sea that forms a splendid harbor. It is certainly the most remarkable and interesting city in Europe, not only on historical grounds, but also because of the many Oriental types of life and character in which it abounds. The principal sights of Constantinople are the Bazaars, Mosques, Tombs, the Seraglio, the offices of the Sublime Porte, the Museum of the Janissaries and the Cemetery of Scutari. The most important mosques are those of St. Sophia, one of the famous edifices of the world; Sulieman, Achmed, Mohammed II. and Eyret. The famous Bazaars are most characteristic of Oriental life. The numberless little shops form a great arch-covered labyrinth of streets, passages and crossways, and display a curious and interesting collection of merchandise, gold and silver smiths' work, jewels and precious stones, arms and armor, fabrics of every kind, embroideries, spices—every article of Oriental and Occi-

CONSTANTINOPLE.—MOSQUE OF ACHMED.

PALESTINE.—A COOK ENCAMPMENT.

dental production it is possible to think of. Another great attraction is the famous Imperial Ottoman Museum, one of the most valuable museums in the world.

During the stay at Constantinople an excursion by steamboats will be made up the Golden Horn, and the "Moltke" will proceed up the Bosphorus for a trip to the Black Sea and return on the day of departure.

THE LEVANT.

Sunday, March 1.—Arrive at **Smyrna** early in the morning, and land to visit the famous Bazaars and other sights, the Tomb of Polycarp, the Acropolis on Mount Pagus, etc.

For passengers wishing to visit the extensive ruins of **Ephesus,** a special train will be arranged to make the trip. Among the sights of Ephesus are the marvellous ruin of the great Temple of Diana, the traditional prison of St. Paul and the tomb of St. Luke. Cost of excursion, $3.50.

AN EASTERN STREET.

The voyage from Constantinople and Smyrna, through the Ægean Sea and among the beautiful islands of the Grecian Archipelago, is one of continuous beauty and interest. The steamer passes Rhodes and Cyprus, islands famous in history and mythology. Charles Dudley Warner, describing the voyage, says: "The view was surpassingly lovely; islands, green and poetic, a coast ever retreating and advancing, as if in coquetry with the blue waves, purple robing the hills—a voyage for poets and lotus eaters."

THE HOLY LAND.

Tuesday, March 3.—Arrive at **Beyrout,** the principal commercial town of Syria, a city of great antiquity, beautifully situated on a bold promontory, with walls three miles in circumference. *(Cook's Office, near Hotel d'Orient.)* Beyrout is famous for its missionary and philanthropic institutions, chief among which is the American Mission, established in 1823. Pleasant excursions may be made to the environs, the chief of which is to the Dog River to view the sculptures cut on the face of the rocks. These are nine in number—three Egyptian and six Assyrian. One of the former is dedicated to Phthah, the god of Memphis; another to Ra, the Sun god; the third records certain expeditions of Sesostris (Rameses II.). The Assyrian sculptures are regarded as the work of Sennacherib, who invaded Syria 701 B. C. On this occasion the steamer makes only a short stay, returning on March 5 for three days. The passengers for the Excursion to Damascus (see page 59) leave the ship here. The steamer sails at midnight for Haifa.

Wednesday, March 4.—A call at **Haifa.** *(Cook's Office, near Hotel Carmel.)* Land passengers for the Tour to Galilee and Samaria, described on page 60, and proceed to Jaffa. On March 8 the steamer returns to Haifa and remains 12 hours.

Wednesday, March 4.—Arrive at noon at **Jaffa,** the ancient Joppa *(Cook's Office, German Colony),* and after visiting Simon's House and other historic places proceed

JAFFA.

by special train to Jerusalem, passing the Plain of Sharon, Ramleh and the mountains of Judea. Jerusalem is reached in three and a half hours.

Notice.—The choice of five days in Egypt and twelve days in the Holy Land, or vice versa, is offered, and the "Moltke" will make a double trip between Palestine and Egypt for this purpose. Passengers must decide which they will take by January 5, 1903. In either case we provide the hotel accommodations.

JERUSALEM.—MOSQUE OF OMAR.

Wednesday, March 4, to Monday, March 9 (or 16). —At **Jerusalem.** *(Cook's Office, D a v i d Street.)* Jerusalem, the Holy City, stands on four hills, once separated by deep valleys, but now partially filled up by the debris of successive destructions of the city. The modern city may be considered as the eighth built on the same spot, and the foundations of the ancient walls are in some places 130 feet below the surface. It is inclosed by walls averaging about 35 feet in height, containing thirty-four towers and eight gates,

PALESTINE.—A COOK PARTY AT JERICHO.

six open and two closed. Among the chief objects and places of interest to be visited are the Church of the Holy Sepulchre, the Garden Tomb, the site of the Temple with the Mosque of Omar, the Via Dolorosa, the House of Caiaphas, Tombs of the Judges, Tombs of the Kings, Solomon's Quarries, the Tomb of David, Garden of Gethsemane, etc.

The party will visit **Bethlehem** and **Bethany** by carriage. Bethlehem is situated on an elongated hill, well cultivated in terraces, and with fertile cornfields in the valley below. On the terraces vines and fig trees flourish in abundance. The great sight of Bethlehem is the Church of the Nativity, built over a cave or grotto in the hillside, universally believed to be the actual place of Our Lord's birth.

Bethany is a prettily situated village amid luxuriant gardens and cornfields, where may be seen the House of Mary and Martha, an old tower called the Castle of Lazarus, and the so-called Tomb of Lazarus. Other excursions may be

BETHANY.

made to the **Dead Sea, Jordan, Jericho**, etc., at a slight extra expense. For other excursions in the Holy Land, Galilee, Samaria, Damascus, etc., see pages 59-65.

Monday, March 9 (or 16).—Leave Jerusalem early in the morning by rail for Jaffa, and sail for Alexandria.

EGYPT.

(Option of Five or Twelve Days in Egypt.)

Tuesday, March 10 (or 17).—Arrive at **Alexandria** at 7 A. M. and proceed by train to Cairo. *(Cook's Office, Rue Cherif Pacha.)* After landing passengers leaving Jaffa on March 9, the steamer returns to that port for those who have decided to remain for 12 days in the Holy Land, returning with these to Alexandria on March 17. Passengers must decide whether they will stay 12 days in Palestine and 5 in Egypt, or 5 days in Palestine and 12 in Egypt, not later than January 5, 1903. In either case we provide the hotel accommodation.

Tuesday, March 10 (or 17), to Sunday, March 22.—To be spent in **Cairo**. *(Cook's Office, near Shepheard's Hotel.)* Backed by its white citadel and the yellow range of the

EGYPT.—THE PYRAMIDS

Mokuttam Hills, the great "Al Cairo," as Milton calls it, the city of Saladin and the Arabian Nights, is an everchanging panorama of life and interest. In the older parts of the city the streets are so narrow as to scarcely admit of two camels passing abreast; its bazaars glow with the richest productions of the looms of the East; its mosques and minarets are apparently innumerable, and its fountains fill the air with an enduring freshness. The crowd of people of every nationality passing hither and thither is perfectly bewildering—a moving mass of white turbans, red fezes, of blue, black, white and yellow garments, while the centre has its lines of camels, donkeys and carriages moving slowly in each direction.

STREET IN CAIRO.

The Minarets of Cairo are the most beautiful of any in the East, towering to an extraordinary height, built of alternate courses of red and white sandstone and ornamented with balconies from which muezzins announce the hour of prayer.

The principal objects of interest in Cairo are the Bazaars, which are intensely interesting; the Dancing Dervishes, the many beautiful Mosques (there are 400 in various stages of preservation), the Citadel, which overlooks the city from a towering rock; the Museum at Gizeh, a perfect treasure house of Egyptian antiquities; Tombs and Cemeteries and the walls of the city. In the environs are the following: The Obelisk of Heliopolis, Ruins of Memphis, the Petrified Forest, the Tombs of the Caliphs and the Pyramids of Ghizeh and Sakkarah.

Arrangements have been perfected for the stay of the party in Cairo that will insure a most satisfactory and enjoyable visit. Many of the principal points of interest will be visited in companies of a suitable number, under the charge of competent guides, carriages being furnished where necessary, for the trip to the Pyramids and the Sphinx, and also for one drive through the city and environs. The small parties will in this way be able to inspect and explore every locality and object of interest worth visiting, including those enumerated above, and all others necessary to give the members of the cruise a thorough knowledge of Cairo and Cairene life. All expenses, fees and backsheesh are provided, including admission to the Pyramid of Gizeh, Sphinx, Museum, etc., but not the extra assistance of Arabs for ascending the Pyramid.

Sunday, March 22.—Leave Cairo for Alexandria. A carriage drive will be provided, visiting the chief sights of this interesting and historic city, Pompey's Pillar, etc. In the afternoon sail for Naples.

STRAITS OF MESSINA.

The ship's course, after leaving Alexandria, lies through the Straits of Messina, between Italy and Sicily, where the ancients located the rock of Scylla and the whirlpool of Charybdis, and passing within sight of the volcanoes of Etna and Stromboli.

ITALY.

Wednesday, March 25, to Monday, March 30. —Arrive at **Naples** on Wednesday. *(Cook's Office, Piazza dei Martiri.)* During the stay of six days the party will be divided into sections for visiting Naples and its vicinity, Pompeii and Rome; accommodations, sightseeing, carriage drives, etc., as stated on page 44, will be furnished at the expense of THOS. COOK & SON.

Naples is the chief city of Southern Italy, splendidly situated on one of the most beautiful bays in the world, and as seen from the sea is one of the loveliest spots in Europe.

— 42 —

On the east Vesuvius raises its isolated summit with its eternal crown of smoke. Herculaneum and Pompeii nestle under its green slopes, and to the west the wide amphitheatre of the town, with its multi-colored buildings and background of green hills. The street life of Naples is a striking and picturesque scene, especially on market days, and it is one of the most important centres in Europe for tourists and travelers. Among the places to be visited are the Museum, the Cathedral of San Genaro, the Royal Palace, Castles of St. Elmo, Capuano, Nuevo, del Carmine, etc., Virgil's Tomb and many churches.

Rome. *(Cook's Offices, 51 Piazza Esedra di Termini and 1b Piazza di Spagna.)* It is impossible to describe in a few lines the attractions of Rome, the "Eternal City." Its antiquities are legion. Among its notable buildings, whose names are known the world over, are the Vatican, St. Peter's, the Capitol, Quirinal, Coliseum, Pantheon, Forum, Lateran, Castle of St. Angelo, Temple of Venus and many

NAPLES.

others. There are over 360 churches, many of them famous for their architectural beauty or the treasures they contain. Rome has a thousand attractions—street life of to-day, its antiquities and endless treasures of Art, and every moment spent within the walls must be full of interest to every one.

The time spent in Italy will be so arranged as to avoid confusion between those sections who leave the party at Naples for the Optional Excursions through Europe and those proceeding on the steamer to Villefranche.

While the sections are in Naples they will sleep on board the Steamship "Moltke"; for the excursion to Pompeii and Rome hotel accommodation will be provided at our expense, and a suitable arrangement of time will be made to allow those passengers who desire to take the Optional Trips to Vesuvius and the Blue Grotto at Capri, but it must be noted that bookings for these optional trips must be made by January 5, 1903, in order that accommodation, which is limited, may be secured. The ascent of Vesuvius is made by the Funicular Railway, the property of THOS. COOK & SON, and the cost of the trip is $5. The visit to Capri is by local steamer, the expense, including the Blue Grotto, being $4; these being extras.

> *In Italy the following accommodation is furnished at the expense of* THOS. COOK & SON: *Transfers to and from the steamer at Naples; a carriage drive in Naples; excursion by rail to Pompeii and Rome, with 4 days' hotel accommodation and one day's carriage drive in Rome; transfers in Rome and the services of experienced Guides and Conductors and an accomplished archaeologist in Rome.*

THE RIVIERA.

Wednesday, April 1, or Thursday, April 2.—The steamer is due to arrive at **Villefranche**, the port of Nice, and visits will be made to **Nice** and **Monte Carlo.** Nice is the chief pleasure resort of the lovely Riviera, a beautiful and interesting city and famous Society resort. Monte Carlo is visited by pleasure seekers and the *elite* of European society on account of its perfect climate and matchless scenery, as well as from the

MONTE CARLO.—THE CASINO.

attractions of the "Cercle des Etrangers," as the gambling establishment is called. At the time of our visit the season will be at its height, and the resorts of the Riviera thronged with Royal and other distinguished personages. The steamer sails from Villefranche for New York at midnight.

Tuesday, April 14, or Wednesday, April 15. }—The steamer is due to arrive at **New York** Tuesday or Wednesday, according to the day of departure from Villefranche.

OPTIONAL RETURNING ROUTES ACROSS EUROPE.

A number of very attractive Optional Routes across Europe, returning to New York by Hamburg-American Line steamers from Cherbourg or Southampton, at exceptionally moderate fares, will be found on pages 67 to 79.

THE NILE.—COOK'S TOURIST STEAMER "RAMESES III."

THE NILE

BY

Cook's First-Class Steamers, Especially Built for the Service, the Finest on the Nile.

The following excursions are Optional, as many members of the Cruise may not be disposed to take them, and the fares are additional to those charged for the Cruise. As only a limited number of passengers can be taken on some of these trips, application must be made when booking for the Cruise, and full payment made by January 5, 1903. Plans can be seen and berths secured now.

THOS. COOK & SON's large fleet of elegant steamers on the Nile, specially designed and constructed for them, and their immense facilities and equipment and large permanent staff enable them to furnish exclusive and superior advantages for Egyptian travel.

In order to obviate any overcrowding or inconvenience, THOS. COOK & SON have arranged for a SPECIAL TRAIN TO LEAVE CAIRO FOR LUXOR EVERY NIGHT, if necessary, during the stay of the party in Egypt.

THE NILE.—PHILÆ.

OPTIONAL NILE EXCURSION No. 1

FROM

Cairo to Memphis, Assiout, Abydos, Denderah, Thebes, Karnak and Luxor.

A Seven-Day Tour, including Five Days on Board One of COOK'S FIRST-CLASS STEAMERS, Specially Reserved for Members of the "Moltke" Cruise.

For passengers spending 12 days in Egypt and 5 in Palestine.

COST OF EXCURSION, including five days' accommodation on the Nile steamer, Cairo to Luxor, and sleeping car returning, accommodation at Luxor, transfers, guides, fees, donkeys for excursions to Memphis, Temples of Sethi and Rameses at Abydos, Thebes, Karnak, etc., first class throughout................................. **$75**

Including the Egyptian Government tax of $5.

DAILY ITINERARY.

Tuesday, March 10, 1903.—The steamship "Moltke" will arrive at **Alexandria** at 7 A. M. Passengers for the Nile will leave by fast express train for **Cairo** and transfer to one of Cook's Tourist Steamers.

The first stoppage after leaving Cairo is made at Bedrachin, where donkeys will be in readiness for the passengers. The site of ancient **Memphis** is now covered with shady groves of picturesque palms, among which recline the two famous colossal statues of Rameses the Great. The necessary time will be allowed for visiting the step pyramid of Sakkarah, Mariette Bey's house; the Serapeum, the Tomb of Tih and the Pyramid of Oonas, opened and cleared at the expense of Thos. Cook & Son. The steamer will proceed for that night as far as Ayat.

Wednesday, March 11.—The steamer will leave Ayat at daylight, and during the day the following places of interest will be passed: The dwarf Pyramid of Maydoom, called

El Kedab, or "the false pyramid;" Wasta, a village of some importance and the railway junction for the Fayoum; Beni-sooef, the chief town of the province; Maghaga, where there is one of the largest sugar manufactories in Upper Egypt; "Gebel-el-Tayr," on the top of which stands a Coptic Convent, and Minieh, a populous Arab town. Shortly after Beni-Hassan is reached.

Thursday, March 12.—Leave Beni-Hassan early in the morning; pass Rodah, where there is an important sugar manufactory; the mountain "Gabel-aboo-faydah" and Manfaloot, to **Assiout**, where the gigantic subsidiary reservoir has been constructed. If time permits, land at Assiout and visit the Bazaars, etc. The steamer proceeds to Aboutig for the night.

THE NILE.—LUXOR.

Friday, March 13.—The steamer passes Sohag, an important place, and Girgeh, reaching Bellianah, the stopping place for Abydos, in the evening.

Saturday, March 14.—An excursion to the magnificent ruins of **Abydos**, thought by many Egyptologists to occupy the site of THIS, the earliest historical city of Egypt, the birthplace of Mena, first king of the first dynasty. It is also the reputed burial place of Osiris, and certainly one of the most ancient places in Egypt.

Visit the Temple of Seti, decorated with the most beautiful sculptures in Egypt, containing the most wonderful genealogical record in the world, the Tablet of Abydos, and the Temple of Rameses II.

The steamer will proceed as far as Dishneh for the night.

Sunday, March 15.—To Keneh, and visit the famous Temple of **Denderah**, on the opposite bank, dedicated to the Egyptian "Venus" Hathor, and so closely associated with the beautiful Cleopatra, to whom much of the fine

THE NILE.—COOK'S EXPRESS STEAMER "CLEOPATRA."

sculpture on the outer walls is due. It is one of the most impressive and best preserved of the ancient buildings of Egypt.

The steamer continues to Luxor the same day.

Sunday, March 15, and Monday, March 16.—At **Luxor,** a famous scenic and health resort, and the site of most of the finest of the remains of ancient Egypt. During the stay donkeys and guides will be provided for visiting and inspecting the chief of these, among which may be mentioned the following: The great Temple of Karnak, with the Avenue of Sphinxes; the Propylæ, the Court, the Great Hall, etc.; the great Sitting Colossi; the Temple of Deir-el-Medeeneh (the judgment hall of Osiris); the Temple of Medinet-Haboo, which was the palace and great Temple of Rameses III.; the Temple of Koorneh; the Tombs of the Kings.

Leave Luxor on Monday evening in sleeping cars for Cairo.

Tuesday, March 17, to Sunday, March 22.—To be spent in **Cairo.** *(Cook's Office, near Shepheard's Hotel.)* The arrangements made for the entertainment of the members at Cairo are described in the Itinerary of the main section on page 40.

THEBES.—SITTING COLOSSI.

OPTIONAL NILE EXCURSION NO. 2

Cairo to Luxor, Thebes, Karnak, Denderah Abydos, Assiout and Memphis.

A Seven-Day Tour, from Cairo to Luxor by Sleeping Car and Four Days on Board One of COOK'S FIRST-CLASS STEAMERS Returning, Specially Reserved for Members of the "Moltke" Cruise.

(The same as Excursion No. 1, but in the reverse direction.)

COST OF EXCURSION, including first class railroad tickets and sleeper from Cairo to Luxor, four days' accommodation on the Nile steamer, transfers, guides, fees, donkeys for Excursions to Memphis, Temples of Sethi and Rameses at Abydos, Thebes, Karnak, etc., first class throughout **$75**

Including the Egyptian Government tax of $5.

DAILY ITINERARY.

The sightseeing, etc., is described in the previous Itinerary.

Tuesday, March 10, to Friday, March 13.—At **Alexandria** and **Cairo**. *(Cook's Office, near Shepheard's Hotel).* Leave Cairo by special train of sleeping cars for Luxor.

Saturday, March 14, to Monday, March 16.—To be spent at **Luxor**, visiting Karnak, Thebes, etc., as previously described. Leave early Monday morning for the trip to Cairo by Cook's Tourist steamer.

Monday, March 16, to Friday, March 20.—On the voyage down the Nile, visiting **Denderah, Abydos, Assiout** and **Memphis**.

Friday, March 20, to Sunday, March 22.—In **Cairo** with the main section. Sightseeing and accommodation as already described on page 40.

OPTIONAL NILE EXCURSION NO. 3

Cairo to Luxor, Edfou, Assouan (First Cataract of the Nile), Philae, Karnak, Thebes, Etc.

A Six-Day Tour, from Cairo to Luxor and Return by Sleeping Car, and from Luxor to Assouan (First Cataract) and Return by One of COOK'S FIRST-CLASS STEAMERS, Specially Reserved for Members of the "Moltke" Cruise.

COST OF EXCURSION, including first class rail and sleeping car from Cairo to Luxor and return, first class steamer Luxor to Assouan and return, guides, donkeys for excursions, fees and all necessary expenses.... **$75**
Including the Egyptian Government tax of $5.

DAILY ITINERARY.

Tuesday, March 10, 1903.—Arrive at **Alexandria** and **Cairo.** Leave Cairo by special train of sleeping cars for Luxor.

Wednesday, March 11.—Arrive at **Luxor** in the morning, and transfer to Cook's special steamer, which proceeds up the river to Edfou, arriving in the evening.

Thursday, March 12.—Visit the celebrated **Temple of Edfou,** one of the most complete and best preserved specimens of the Egyptian Temple in existence. It is dedicated to Horus, and was commenced in 237 B. C. by Ptolemy III. The length of the Temple is 450 feet, and the entrance is by a double Pylon 250 feet wide and 115 feet high, from the top of which a magnificent view is obtained. Within is the great Court containing a colonnade of 32 columns, leading to the Vestibule with 12 columns and the Hypostyle Hall and other chambers, the Sanctuary, many passages, etc. The whole edifice contains many inscriptions of the greatest interest. After visiting the Temple the party embarks for Assouan, arriving in the afternoon.

Friday, March 13.—**Assouan** is an important town, where a considerable garrison is stationed, 585 miles from Cairo, the scene of many improvements brought about since British occupation. There are some interesting Bazaars, but the importance of the locality to tourists is owing to the many beautiful historic remains. The chief of these is the **Island of Philae**, the Pearl of Egypt, containing many ruins, the principal being the Temple of Isis, and the smaller Temple known as Pharaoh's Bed. On the return to Assouan, the steamer starts on the downward voyage to Luxor.

Saturday, March 14, and Sunday, March 15.—Arrive at **Luxor** on Saturday, and devote the two days to visiting **Thebes, Karnak** and other places of interest as outlined for Nile Tour No. 1. Leave on Sunday night for Cairo by sleeping cars.

Monday, March 16, to Sunday, March 22.—In **Cairo** with the main section. Sightseeing and accommodation as already described on page 40.

EGYPT.—THE SUEZ CANAL.

OPTIONAL NILE EXCURSION No. 4

Cairo to Luxor, Edfou, Assouan (First Cataract of the Nile), Philae, Karnak, Thebes, Etc.

A Six-Day Tour, from Cairo to Luxor and Return by Sleeping Car, and from Luxor to Assouan (First Cataract) and Return by One of COOK'S FIRST-CLASS STEAMERS, Specially Reserved for Members of the "Moltke" Cruise.

This excursion is practically the same as Nile Excursion No. 3, with the exception of the arrangement of the dates, which have been changed to avoid crowding.

COST OF EXCURSION, including first class rail and sleeping car from Cairo to Luxor and return, first class steamer Luxor to Assouan and return, guides, donkeys for excursions, fees and all necessary expenses......... **$75** Including the Egyptian Government tax of $5.

DAILY ITINERARY.

Tuesday, March 10, 1903.—Arrive at **Alexandria** and **Cairo**.

Wednesday, March 11, and Thursday, March 12.—In **Cairo** with main section of the party. Leave Thursday evening by special train of sleeping cars for Luxor.

Friday, March 13, and Saturday, March 14.—At **Luxor**. Visit **Thebes, Karnak**, etc., as described on page 51. Leave on Saturday by COOK's special steamer for Assouan.

Sunday, March 15.—Visit the **Temple of Edfou**, and continue to Assouan.

Monday, March 16.—At Assouan. Visit **Philae** and the Cataract.

Tuesday, March 17.—Leave for Luxor, arriving late in the afternoon. Leave Luxor by special train of sleeping cars for Cairo.

Wednesday, March 18, to Sunday, March 22. described on page 40. —To be spent in **Cairo** with main section of party. Sightseeing and accommodations as

OPTIONAL NILE EXCURSION NO. 5.

Cairo to Luxor, Karnak, Thebes, Denderah, Abydos, Assiout and Memphis.

A Six-Day Tour, from Cairo to Luxor by Sleeping Car and Four Days' Accommodation on One of
COOK'S FIRST-CLASS STEAMERS
Returning, Specially Reserved for
Members of the "Moltke"
Cruise.

COST OF EXCURSION, including first class rail and sleeper from Cairo to Luxor, steamer from Luxor to Cairo, with board, guides, donkeys for excursions, fees, etc. **$75**
Including the Egyptian Government tax of $5.

DAILY ITINERARY.

Tuesday, March 10, to Sunday, March 15. —In **Cairo.** Sightseeing and accommodations as described on page 40.

Leave Cairo on Sunday night by special train of sleeping cars for Luxor.

Monday, March 16, and Tuesday, March 17.—At **Luxor.** Visit **Karnak, Thebes,** etc., as described in itinerary of Nile Tour No. 1.

Wednesday, March 18, to Sunday, March 22.—Leave early on Wednesday morning, and proceed down the river to Cairo, visiting **Denderah, Abydos, Assiout** and **Memphis,** as outlined for Nile Tour No. 1.

Sunday, March 22.—Arrive at **Cairo,** and join main section of party.

EGYPT.—THE SPHINX.

A COOK ENCAMPMENT AT BAALBEC.

OPTIONAL SIDE TRIPS

TO

DAMASCUS, GALILEE, SAMARIA, DEAD SEA, JORDAN, Etc.

Members of the Cruise desiring to take any of these Optional Side Trips, must decide when booking, paying a deposit of $5.00, and full payment will be required by January 5, 1903.

THOS. COOK & SON'S large resident staff and immense equipment in the Holy Land enable them to offer such advantages to tourists as can be obtained in no other manner, and to offer these short Tours at the absolutely unprecedentedly low rates quoted.

Circumstances over which we have no control, such as the hour of arrival of steamer, etc., may necessitate some slight changes in the arrangement of the dates for these Extension Trips, but ample margins of time are allowed, so that the Trips may be fully carried out, although not on the exact days stated.

Optional Side Trip

TO

DAMASCUS.

COST OF EXCURSION, including railroad tickets, transfers, hotel accommodation for the stated time, and guides **$25**

Tuesday, March 3.—Arrive at **Beyrout** at 1 P. M. *(Cook's Office, near Hotel d'Orient.)* Visit the Bazaars and other places of interest, including the American Mission. (See page 35.)

Wednesday, March 4.—Leave Beyrout by morning train for Damascus, ascending the Lebanon to some 4,900 feet above sea level en route.

Thursday, March 5.—In **Damascus,** the oldest city in the world—older even than Abraham, whose servant came from here. It is to-day a true Oriental city, with mosques, minarets and domes and famous Bazaars, and is surrounded with verdure and fruitful gardens. Among the more prominent points of interest are the "Street called Straight," the house of Ananias, the house of Judas, the Leper's Hospital (the reputed site of Naaman's house).

Friday, March 6.—Return by train to Beyrout. The steamer remains at Beyrout until 9 A. M. on Sunday, March 8, but owing to the possibility of trains being delayed by snow on the mountains it is best to leave an ample margin of time.

ONE OF COOK'S DRAGOMANS.

Optional Side Trip
TO
GALILEE.

By Carriage from Haifa to Nazareth, Tiberias and Return.

COST OF EXCURSION, including carriages and all expenses **$28**

Wednesday, March 4.—Land at **Haifa.** *(Cook's Office, near Hotel Carmel.)* Visits may be made to Mount Carmel, the scene of Elijah's sacrifice, with its famous Monastery and the School of the Prophets.

Thursday, March 5.—Leave by carriage for **Nazareth,** a pleasant drive, passing by the Heroosheth of the Gentiles and Sheich Braik, the old Roman Caves and cemeteries. At Nazareth visit the Church of the Annunciation, the Holy Grotto, the Workshop of Joseph, etc.

Friday, March 6.—Proceed to **Tiberias,** on the Lake of Galilee, passing Cana of Galilee and the Mount of Beatitudes. Weather permitting, a sail on the Lake will be enjoyed, and an excursion made to Capernaum, etc.

Saturday, March 7.—The morning will be spent in and around Tiberias; in the afternoon return to Nazareth.

Sunday, March 8.—Return to Haifa and embark on steamer.

SHEIKH RASCHID OF THE JORDAN VALLEY.

PALESTINE.—VIEW OF A COOK ENCAMPMENT.

Optional Tour from Haifa

TO

JERUSALEM, THROUGH GALILEE AND SAMARIA.

Nine-Day Tour.

COST OF EXCURSION........................ **$60**

Including all necessary accommodation and travelling expenses.

Wednesday, March 4.—In **Haifa.**

Thursday, March 5.—By carriage to **Nazareth.**

Friday, March 6.—To Tiberias.

Saturday, March 7.—At **Tiberias,** and return to Nazareth.

To this point the Tour is identical with the previous one, and the descriptions, sightseeing, etc., are also the same.

Sunday, March 8.—Day of Rest at **Nazareth.**

Monday, March 9.—Travel by way of Nain, round Little Hermon, Shunem and Jezreel to Jenin (Engannim) on the Plain of Esdraelon, which is surrounded by mountains—on the south, the Hills of Samaria; west, Mount Carmel; northwest, the Hills of Galilee, and northeast, the mountains of Gilboa.

Tuesday, March 10.—Journey to Dothan, and through fertile hills and valleys to Samaria.

Wednesday, March 11.—By way of Nablous, the ancient Shechem, Joseph's Tomb, Jacob's Well, and over the ridge of Shiloh to Sinjil.

Thursday, March 12.—Travel to Bethel, thence to **Jerusalem,** over Mount Scopus and the Tombs of the Kings. At Jerusalem connection is made with the party landing at Jaffa.

Optional Side Trip from Jerusalem

TO

THE DEAD SEA, THE JORDAN AND JERICHO.

COST OF EXCURSION............................ **$10**

Including all necessary accommodation and travelling expenses.

First Day.—Leave Jerusalem by carriage or horseback for **Jericho**. Pass round the city, and obtain a good view of the city walls, the Damascus Gate, the Grotto of Jeremiah, the Valley of Jehoshaphat, etc. The route makes a circuit of the city, and, passing the Garden of Gethsemane, turns off near the Tomb of Absalom, across the slope of the Mount of Olives to **Bethany**, where the traditional site of the house of Mary and Martha may be seen. Then across the wilderness of Judea, past the Apostle's Spring and the Inn of the Good Samaritan, to the gorge of the Cherith, thence to **Jericho**, situated on the Plain of the Jordan, in view of the Dead Sea, the Mountains of Moab, the course of the Jordan, the Mount of Temptation and the Valley of the Jordan as far as the snowy Peak of Hermon. Lunch at Jericho.

After lunch proceed across the Plain of the Jordan to the **Dead Sea**, in view of Mount Nebo and Mount Pisgah. This strange body of water, which lies 1,292 feet below the level of the Mediterranean, is intensely salt, and no life exists in its waters. In clear weather the scenery presented by its waters and the surrounding mountains is beautiful. There will be an opportunity for those who desire to bathe in the curiously buoyant waters to do so. Then travel to the **Fords of the Jordan**, where many visitors bathe in the sacred waters, this being the reputed scene of the Baptism of Our Lord. Return to Jericho for the night.

Second Day.—Return to Jerusalem, enjoying a magnificent view of the city from the Mount of Olives.

Optional Side Trip from Jerusalem
TO
HEBRON.

COST OF EXCURSION............ .... **$3.50**

The route from Jerusalem passes the **Valley of Hinnom,** the traditional **Well of the Magi** and the **Tomb of Rachel.** Thence to the three **Pools of Solomon,** which lie in a small valley near a castle; then past the Shrine of Abraham to **Hebron,** a town of great antiquity, where tradition places the cave of Macpelah.

SHEIKH FALLAH OF MOAB AND THE BALKAA.

ACROSS EUROPE.

Optional Route No. 1. Leaving the Steamer at Villefranche, April 1 or 2.

Visiting Monte Carlo, Nice, Cannes, Marseilles, Lyons, Paris and Cherbourg.

COST OF TOUR **$45**

DAILY ITINERARY.

Thursday, April 2, 1903.—Travel by rail to **Monte Carlo** and **Nice**, two charming society resorts of the famous Riviera. *(Cook's Offices: Monte Carlo, Credit Lyonnais; Nice, 16 Avenue Massena.)*

Friday, April 3.—From Nice to **Cannes,** the most aristocratic of the Winter Cities of the Riviera, most delightfully situated. Thence to **Marseilles,** an important French seaport. *(Cook's Office, 11b Rue Noailles.)*

Saturday, April 4.—Travel to Paris by day express.

Sunday, April 5, to Thursday, April 9.—To be spent in **Paris.** *(Cook's Office, 1 Place de l'Opera.)* Carriages will be furnished on one day. The principal interesting places and objects in and around the city are the Invalides and Tomb of Napoleon I.; the Palace, Gardens, and Park of Versailles, Gardens and Park of Trocadéro, the Palace of the Tuileries, Cathedral of Notre Dame, etc. Cook's Guide to Paris will be found very useful.

Friday, April 10.—Take the express train for Cherbourg and embark by Hamburg-American Line twin-screw express steamship for New York.

Friday, April 17.—Arrive at **New York.**

SWITZERLAND.—LAKE OF LUCERNE.

The Fare Includes
first class railroad tickets for route as stated; accommodation at first class hotels, consisting of breakfast, lunch and table d'hote dinner; transfers between stations and hotels, carriage drive in Paris; conveyance of 56 pounds of baggage on the Continent; fees to hotel servants, railroad porters and guards, and the services of a competent conductor from Villefranche to Cherbourg.

ACROSS EUROPE.

Optional Route No. 2. Leaving the Steamer at Villefranche, April 1 or 2.

Visiting Monte Carlo, Nice, Genoa, Milan, St. Gothard, Lucerne, Bale, Paris, Cherbourg.

COST OF TOUR.............................. $56

DAILY ITINERARY.

Thursday, April 2, 1903.—To **Monte Carlo** and **Nice** by rail, as previously described.

ITALY.

Friday, April 3.—Travel to **Genoa**. *(Cook's Office, 17 Piazza della Meridiana.)* Genoa is a city of palaces, and contains a handsome Cathedral. Proceed later to Milan. *(Cook's Office, 7 Via A Manzoni.)* Milan is famous for its Cathedral, one of the wonders of the world.

Saturday, April 4.—Spend the morning at **Milan**, a carriage drive being provided. In the afternoon take train for Lucerne. The railroad touches the shores of Lakes Como and Lugano, and thence over the celebrated St. Gothard railway to the Lake of Lucerne. The journey is crowded with visions of gorges, torrents, snowy peaks, inaccessible heights, cascades, bright green slopes where herds of cattle graze, and deep, fertile valleys where picturesque villages sleep in the shadow of rugged mountains.

PARIS.

SWITZERLAND.

Sunday, April 5.—In **Lucerne.** *(Cook's Office, Schwanenplatz.)* Visit the chief points of interest, Thorwaldsen's immortal work, "The Lion of Lucerne," the Glacial Garden, the old bridges, etc. Lucerne lies picturesquely on the Lake of Lucerne, at the afflux of the Reuss. Its situation, surrounded by low hills, facing the Rigi and Pilatus, and the snow-clad Alps of Uri and Engelberg, is one of surpassing beauty.

Monday, April 6.—Travel from Lucerne to Paris via Bale.

FRANCE.

Tuesday, April 7, to Friday, April 10.—To be spent in **Paris.** *(Cook's Office, 1 Place de l'Opera.)* Carriages will be furnished on one day. The principal places and objects in and around the city are the Invalides and Tomb of Napoleon I., the Palace, Gardens, and Park of Versailles; St. Cloud. Sèvres and its famous porcelain manufactory, Palace of the Trocadéro, the Palace of the Tuileries, Cathedral of Notre Dame, etc. Cook's Guide to Paris will be found very useful.

Friday, April 10.—Leave by express train for Cherbourg, and embark by Hamburg-American Line twin-screw express steamship for New York.

Friday, April 17.—Arrive at **New York.**

The Fare Includes

first class railroad tickets for route as stated; accommodation at first class hotels, consisting of breakfast, lunch and table d'hote dinner; transfers between stations and hotels, carriage drives at Milan and Paris; conveyance of 56 pounds of baggage on the Continent; fees to hotel servants, railroad porters and guards, and the services of a competent conductor from Villefranche to Cherbourg.

ITALY.—BRIDGE OF THE CÆSARS, ROME.

ACROSS EUROPE.

Optional Route No. 3. Leaving the Steamer at Naples, March 25.

Visiting Naples, Rome, Florence, Venice, Milan, Lucerne, Paris and Cherbourg.

COST OF TOUR.................................. **$90**

DAILY ITINERARY.

ITALY.

Wednesday, March 25, and Thursday, March 26, 1903.—In **Naples.** *(Cook's Office, Piazza dei Martiri.)* A carriage drive will be provided and **Pompeii** visited.

Friday, March 27, to Monday, March 30.—In **Rome.** *(Cook's Offices, 51 Piazza Esedra di Termini, and 1b Piazza di Spagna.)* A carriage drive will be provided. The sightseeing in Naples and Rome is described in the Itinerary of the main section of the Cruise.

Monday, March 30.—Leave Rome by afternoon express train for Florence, arriving the same evening.

Tuesday, March 31.—In **Florence.** *(Cook's Office, 10 Via Tornabuoni.)* The city, the home of Dante, Michael Angelo, Savonarola and the Medici family, is externally very much what it was in the days of its greatness. The Grand Duomo, Giotto's Campanile, the Palazzo Vecchio, the Bargello, are full of memories of those mediæval days. Leave by afternoon train for Venice.

Wednesday, April 1, and Thursday, April 2.—In **Venice,** "Queen of the Adriatic." *(Cook's Office, Piazza dei Leoncini, Piazza San Marco.)* The canals are its streets, the gondola the vehicle. The Grand Canal, lined with palaces, is the Broadway of the city. Three bridges cross it, one of which is the famous Rialto.

SWITZERLAND.—SCENE IN THE ALPS.

Among the places of greatest interest are the Square of St. Mark; the Cathedral, unrivalled among the buildings of Europe for richness of material and decorations; the Palace of the Doges, Rialto, Bridge of Sighs and Church of Santa Maria da Salute.

Gondolas for sightseeing provided on one day. Leave by afternoon express train on Thursday for **Milan**.

Friday, April 3.—The morning to be spent in **Milan**. *(Cook's Office, 7 Via A. Manzoni.)* The Cathedral is noted as one of the wonders of the world. Leave by afternoon train for Lucerne by the famous St. Gothard Railway, through most romantic scenery.

SWITZERLAND.

Saturday, April 4, and **Sunday, April 5.**—In **Lucerne**. *(Cook's Office, Schwanenplatz.)* Visit the chief points of interest, Thorwaldsen's immortal work, "The Lion of Lucerne," the Glacial Garden, the old bridges, etc. Lucerne lies picturesquely on the Lake of Lucerne, at the afflux of the Reuss. Its situation, surrounded by low hills, facing the Rigi and Pilatus, and the snow-clad Alps of Uri and Engelberg, is one of surpassing beauty.

Monday, April 6.—By day train to Paris.

PARIS.

Tuesday, April 7, to **Thursday, April 9.**—To be spent in **Paris**. *(Cook's Office, 1 Place de l'Opera.)* Carriages will be furnished on one day. The principal interesting places and objects in and around the city are the Invalides and Tomb of Napoleon I., the Palace, Gardens, and Park of Versailles, Gardens and Park of the Trocadéro, the Palace of the Tuileries, Cathedral of Notre Dame, etc. Cook's Guide to Paris will be found very useful.

Friday, April 10.—Travel by express train to Cherbourg, and embark on Hamburg-American Line twin-screw steamship for New York.

Friday, April 17.—Arrive at **New York**.

ENGLAND.—THE TOWER BRIDGE, LONDON.

The Fare Includes

first class railroad tickets for route as stated; accommodation at first class hotels, consisting of breakfast, lunch and table d'hote dinner; transfers between stations and hotels; carriage drives in Naples, Rome and Paris, gondola excursion in Venice; conveyance of 56 pounds of baggage on the Continent; fees to hotel servants, railroad porters and guards, and the services of a competent conductor from Naples to Cherbourg.

ACROSS EUROPE.

Optional Route No. 4. Leaving Steamer at Naples, March 25.

Visiting Naples, Rome, Florence, Venice, Milan, Lucerne, Paris, London and Southampton.

COST OF TOUR................................. **$130**

DAILY ITINERARY

The route as far as Paris is identical with that outlined for Optional Route No. 3, so descriptions of the places visited are not repeated here.

ITALY.

Wednesday, March 25, to Friday, March 27, 1903.—In **Naples.** *(Cook's Office, Piazza dei Martiri.)* Carriage drive on one day, and excursion to Pompeii.

Saturday, March 28, to Tuesday, March 31.—In **Rome.** *(Cook's Offices, 51 Piazza Esedra di Termini, and 1b Piazza di Spagna.)* Carriage drive on one day. Leave by afternoon train on Tuesday for Florence.

Wednesday, April 1, and **Thursday, April 2.** —In **Florence.** *(Cook's Office, 10 Via Tornabuoni.)* Leave by afternoon train on Thursday for Venice.

Friday, April 3, and **Saturday, April 4.** —In **Venice.** *(Cook's Office, Piazza dei Leoncini, Piazza San Marco.)* Gondola excursion on one day. Leave on Saturday afternoon for Milan.

Sunday, April 5.—In **Milan.** *(Cook's Office, 7 Via A. Manzoni.)*

Monday, April 6.—By the St. Gothard route to Lucerne.

Tuesday, April 7.—In **Lucerne.** *(Cook's Office, Schwanenplatz.)*

PARIS.

Wednesday, April 8.—Travel to Paris.

Thursday, April 9, to **Sunday, April 12.** —In **Paris.** *(Cook's Office, 1 Place de l'Opera.)* Carriage drive on one day.

Monday, April 13.—Leave Paris by day service, via Dieppe and Newhaven, for London.

ENGLAND.

Tuesday, April 14, to **Friday, April 17.** —To be spent in **London.** *(Cook's Chief Office, Ludgate Circus.)* Carriages will be provided on one day. The many points of interest include the Tower, Houses of Parliament, British Museum, Westminster Abbey, St. Paul's Cathedral, National Gallery, the Parks, Thames Embankment and other points of interest in and around the city.

Friday, April 17.—Leave London for Southampton, and embark by Hamburg-American Line twin-screw express steamship for New York.

Friday, April 24.—Arrive at **New York.**

The Fare Includes

first class railroad tickets for route as stated; accommodation at first class hotels, consisting of breakfast, lunch and table d'hote dinner; transfers between stations and hotels; carriage drives in Naples, Rome, Paris and London, gondola excursion in Venice; conveyance of 56 pounds of baggage on the Continent; fees to hotel servants, railroad porters and guards, and the services of a competent conductor from Naples to Southampton.

VENICE.—THE RIALTO.

COOK'S
TOURS TO EUROPE
All Expenses Included

SEASON 1903.

OUR arrangements for 1903 are now completed, and contain the most elaborate, comprehensive and perfect system for visiting Europe ever constructed. These arrangements embody the results of 62 years' continuous experience in the organization and management of tours everywhere in the world. The position in which the firm of THOS. COOK & SON stands is absolutely unique. Travelers under our arrangements are assured all the advantages, conveniences and protection which the presence of the competent salaried staff of the firm in all parts of the world provides.

In addition to our arrangements for personally conducted travel we have, for those intending to "go it alone," tickets to every available spot under the sun, and all holders of these are entitled to the services of our assistants, interpreters, etc., throughout the world, free.